FAMILY LIFE IN
The Second World War

NIGEL SMITH

HODDER
Wayland

an imprint of Hodder Children's Books

FAMILY LIFE SERIES:
Medieval Britain
Roman Britain
Saxon Britain
Second World War
Tudors & Stuarts
Victorian Britain

Series design: Pardoe Blacker Ltd
Editors: Sarah Doughty and Katie Orchard
Production controller: Carol Stevens

First published in Great Britain in 1998 by
Wayland (Publishers) Ltd
Reprinted in 2000 by Hodder Wayland,
an imprint of Hodder Children's Books

© Hodder Wayland 1998

British Library Cataloguing in Publication Data
Smith, Nigel
  Family Life in the Second World War. – (Family Life Series)
    I. Title II. Series
    306.850941

ISBN 0 7502 2303 0

Printed and bound by G. Canale & C.S.p.A, Turin, Italy

Hodder Children's Books
A division of Hodder Headline
338 Euston Road
London NW1 3BH

Cover pictures: A family listening to the war news on the radio, a ration book and a gas mask.

Picture acknowledgements
The publishers would like to thank the following organizations for allowing their pictures to be reproduced in this book: Getty Images 8 (bottom),9, 10 (bottom), 16 (top), 21, 23, 25 (top and bottom), 27 (top and bottom), 28 (left), 29; The Imperial War Museum 6, 7 (top), 8 (top), 11, 12 (top and bottom), 18, 19 (bottom), 28 (right); Kent Messenger Group 10 (top); The London Transport Museum 15 (top); The Newhaven Fort Collection *cover*, 7 (bottom), 13 (top and middle), 22 (bottom), 30 (bottom); Popperfoto *cover*, 4 (top), 5, 14, 16 (bottom), 17 (bottom), 19 (top), 20 (top), 24; Topham Picture Source 17 (top). The commissioned pictures from the Newhaven Fort Collection were photographed by APM Studios. The artwork is by Peter Dennis 13 (bottom). The remaining pictures are from the Wayland Picture Library.

CONTENTS

SAYING GOODBYE

On 3 September 1939, the Prime Minister, Neville Chamberlain, told the British people over the radio that they were at war with **Nazi** Germany. The war changed everything. For most people the worst part was the break-up of families and the separation from the people they loved and from their homes. A popular wartime song was 'We'll Meet Again', but people worried that they would not see some of their family and friends again. One woman remembers:

'We were in the room listening to the broadcast. I remember my small niece aged about eight saying brightly, "Do you think Daddy will get killed?" We just felt pretty awful.'

'Cheer up! I'll soon be home again.' This soldier says goodbye to his wife and baby at the start of the war. No one knew the war would last for six years.

*These small children are being **evacuated** to the safety of the countryside. Many children were too young to understand why they were being sent away.*

Almost at once, thousands of men left their homes to join the armed forces. All men between the ages of eighteen and forty-one had to join up unless their job was vital to the war effort. In the end 7 ½ million men were **conscripted**. Many of them were not to see their families until the end of the war, and some never returned.

EVACUATION

The government was worried that many **civilians** might be killed or injured by German bombing, so they set up an evacuation scheme to move children out of danger areas such as London and other cities. At the start of the war 1 ½ million children were evacuated from their homes and sent to live with strangers in the countryside, where they would be safe. Families and single women in the safe areas were ordered to take in evacuees whether they wanted to or not. The children were loaded on to trains with only the clothes and possessions that they could carry. As mothers and children said goodbye, they had no idea how long they would be apart.

Special trains took these parents to visit their children. But the visits were only short and a few hours later there were sad goodbyes as they left their children behind.

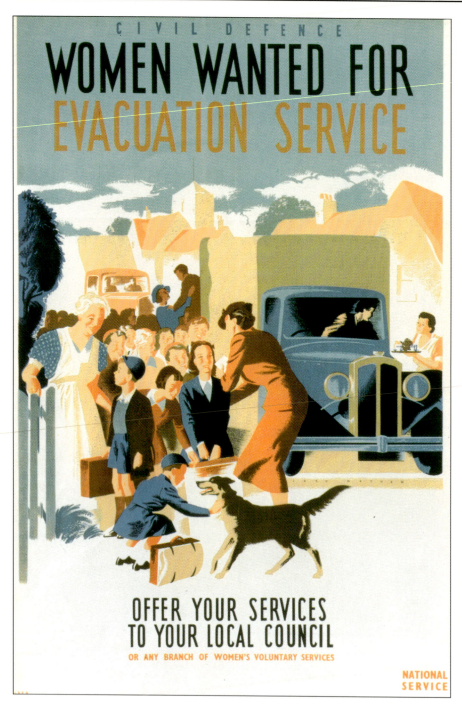

SETTLING DOWN

Some city schools were moved into country hotels and large houses. But most evacuees were sent to village schools, where they probably felt quite out of place. It was very difficult for children who were missing their parents and friends to settle down to live with complete strangers. Some very young children became confused over who their real mother was. Many city children hated the countryside. Some of the poorest children from city **slums** horrified the people they were staying with, who often found it hard to understand the way the children spoke, and were shocked by their rude language.

LIVING ABROAD

A few better-off parents sent their children to live in the USA and Canada, well away from any bombing. Americans called them 'Bundles from Britain'. But the journey was dangerous, because German submarines often attacked passenger ships. Many children died when a refugee ship, the *Empress of Britain*, was sunk.

It must have been very difficult for parents to follow the advice in this leaflet. After visiting their children they are told they must leave them behind.

WHEN YOU VISIT YOUR CHILD IN THE COUNTRY

YOU CAN HELP the housewife with whom your child is billeted by making things as easy as possible for her during your visit. She will not expect to have to provide you with meals. You can give her a welcome rest if you take your child out for the day.

YOU CAN HELP by examining your child's clothes and boots and shoes in order to find out whether they need seeing to. You will naturally wish to do everything you can to keep your child properly clothed and shod. This is an opportunity for you to see for yourself whether anything is needed.

YOU CAN HELP by doing everything you can to encourage your child to stay in the country for safety's sake. DO NOT BRING YOUR CHILD HOME WITH YOU WHEN YOU RETURN.

At first the Germans did not bomb cities and some mothers wanted their children to come home. In this poster, the government warned that this was what Hitler wanted them to do!

RE-EVACUATION

Mothers missed their children and, after a few months when there had been no bombing, some parents brought their children home although the government warned them not to. When the heavy bombing of late 1940 started, many of the children that had been brought home had to be evacuated again. But throughout the war some children stayed with their families in areas that were bombed.

LIFE GOES ON

KEEP DEATH OFF THE ROAD
CARELESSNESS KILLS

For many husbands and wives, the great changes in their lives caused by the war were difficult to bear. Young couples were separated and sometimes they lost their home, either because of bombing, or because the wife left on her own could not afford to keep it. Newly married couples were often not able to set up their own home or have children until the war was over.

*(Left) This grim poster of a widow reminds everyone to be careful on the roads during the **black-out**.*

(Below) These workmen painted black and white stripes on lamposts and even trees so that they would show up better in the black-out.

The separation of families at a time when everyone was in danger caused a great deal of anxiety. Parents worried that their children might be hurt or even killed. Wives were anxious about their husbands who were away fighting the enemy. Those in the armed forces worried that their homes and families might be bombed. People were always longing for news of their loved ones, but letters were often delayed. So civilians on the '**Home Front**' had to cope with these worries as well as many new hardships.

THE BLACK-OUT

Ordinary daily life became very difficult. The most hated of all the **emergency** regulations was the black-out. It was very important to prevent German aircraft from identifying targets, so all street lights were turned off and cars could show only a tiny beam of light. Everybody's windows had to be covered at night with heavy black-out material, and lights had to be turned off before you opened the door so that no crack of light would show.

(Left) Even though there is a war on, workers and their families sit down to enjoy a concert in a bomb-site in Chelsea in August, 1942.

The edges of pavements were painted white, but even so there were many serious road accidents. In the first four months of the war, more than 2,000 people were killed in road accidents. The usual number in peacetime would have been about 300. More people drowned because they fell off bridges or into new ponds provided for firefighting.

During the war, all adults had to carry identity cards. These soldiers are checking the identities of shoppers to make sure they are not German spies.

German bombing caused terrible damage and many deaths. This London bus has fallen into a bomb crater after an air raid in 1940. The people on the bus might have been killed.

TRAVEL

Trains were needed to move soldiers and military equipment. People were asked not to make journeys unless they were really necessary. No one went on outings or holidays.

Travelling anywhere during the war was very difficult. For most of the war there was no petrol for private cars. Road signs were removed to confuse the Germans if they invaded. If you tried to ask anyone the way, you could be mistaken for a German **spy**! Many people used bicycles but, without any lights, they were dangerous after dark. There were no family holidays, and it was usually difficult even for people to visit their relatives.

Railway services were cut back, as the movement of soldiers was thought to be much more important. The Germans frequently bombed railway lines and stations. Commuters struggling into London found they spent more time travelling than being at work. One passenger described a typical train:

'I remember seeing many people sitting on the laps of others. Some trains got so packed that people actually had to climb in and out of the carriages through the windows. Some of the mothers would even put their children in the luggage racks.'

Buses were overcrowded, and the drivers faced a very difficult job during the black-out, especially in bad or foggy weather. Quite a few drivers and conductors were killed or injured by bombs.

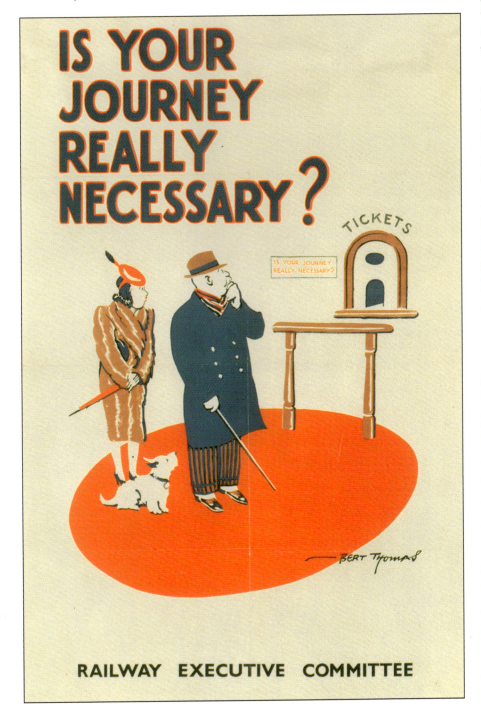

IS YOUR JOURNEY REALLY NECESSARY?

TICKETS

RAILWAY EXECUTIVE COMMITTEE

FOOD RATIONING

There were serious shortages of just about everything, and shopping became a daily nightmare. Mothers worried that their growing children were not eating enough. The government set up a strict system of **rationing** to make certain that everybody got their fair share of foods that were scarce. People would queue for hours, even during an air raid, and then the shop might not have enough for everyone. If anyone complained, the usual reply was, 'Don't you know there's a war on!'

People had to **improvise**. Coffee was made from dried acorns, and cakes were made without eggs. Some people broke the law by buying things that were not available in the shops at higher prices on the 'black market'.

Shoppers got fed up with having to queue. If there wasn't a queue outside a shop, then it probably did not have anything left to sell. This wartime painting shows a typical queue outside a fish shop.

Even Father Christmas was used to tell people that they should lend their war savings to help the war effort. The government needed the money to buy weapons and ships from other countries.

CLOTHING

Clothing too was in short supply and rationed, so that 'make do and mend' became the new slogan. Pillowcases were made into baby clothes, and a father's old trousers might become a skirt for his daughter. Old parachutes were made into blouses and night-dresses. To save material, men's jackets had fake pockets and trousers had no turn-ups. Many women painted their legs with shoe polish so they looked as if they had stockings on. Instead of lipstick they tried cooked beetroot juice!

AVOIDING WASTE

People were continually told, 'Above all avoid waste and so save shipping' so Britain would not have to import more goods. Baths were only meant to be had once a week, and then with just five inches (12.5 cm) of water! People felt they had a duty to obey these rules and so help to win the war.

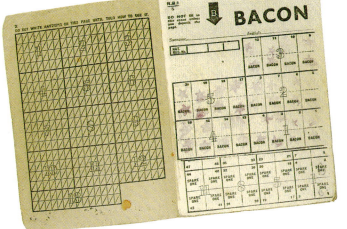

Everybody had ration books like these. Putting up with shortages of food and other everyday items made life very uncomfortable.

FOOD RATIONING							
One week's ration allowance for one person:							
One egg	Margarine (2 oz)	Cooking fat (2 oz)	Tea (2 oz)	Sugar (8 oz)	Cheese (1 oz)	Bacon and ham (4 oz)	Meat (Value of 1 shilling 2d)

In September 1940 began one of the worst times for civilians in Britain. Adolf Hitler ordered the German air force to bomb London and other large cities. This was the **Blitz** that Hitler hoped would force Britain to surrender. The whole country became a battlefield.

Many families slept in an Anderson shelter like this one in their back garden. They were small, and cold in winter. It must have been frightening to be in one of these shelters during an air raid by German bombers.

AIR RAID SHELTERS

Warning of the approach of bombers was given by air raid sirens. As the sirens made their dreadful wailing noise, people stopped what they were doing and quickly took shelter. A few families had built their own **Anderson shelters** in the back garden. These were small, but far more comfortable than the large, crowded public shelters. Night after night the German bombers bombed the city. For seventy-five out of seventy-six nights after 7 September 1940, London was bombed.

UNDERGROUND SHELTERS

Thousands of people living in London sheltered in the underground stations. Mattresses covered the platform, and people even slept on the escalators. One man remembers:

'The constant worry was whether we would find a space for that night.'

With so many people jammed together, the smell was awful, and the noise of hundreds of people snoring took some getting used to. The shelters were cold, and children curled up as close as they could to their mothers. Buckets had to be used as toilets. People took as many of their possessions as they could manage in case their house was destroyed. Sometimes people sang songs to entertain themselves and to help everyone forget the danger. When the 'All Clear' sounded, usually around 6 am, they went up to see the terrible damage that had been done.

SHELTERERS' BEDDING

The practice of shaking bedding over the platforms, tracks and in the subways is strictly forbidden

These families tried to sleep night after night in bunk beds at Holborn underground station. People felt safe underground where they could not hear the sound of German bombers.

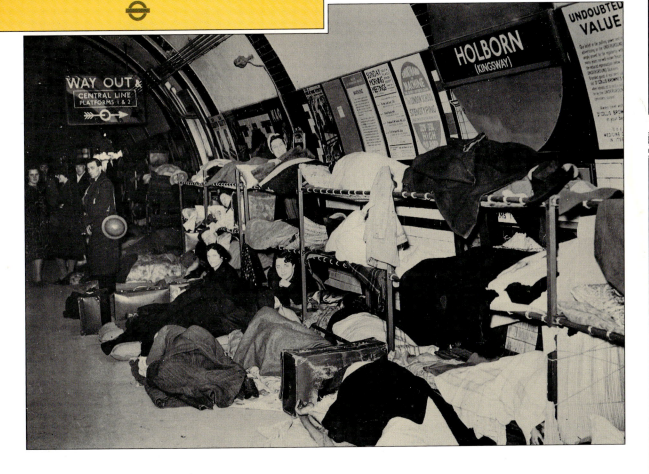

These people are exhausted after many nights away from their homes. They trekked into the countryside to keep their families safe whilst the cities were bombed.

NIGHT-TIME

Some people trudged out every evening from their town into the nearby countryside. They slept where they could and the next morning made their way back to see if their homes were still in one piece. They called it 'trekking'.

The constant noise of bombers, explosions and anti-aircraft gunfire made the Blitz a terrifying experience. People dreaded night-time, when they knew the enemy would return. For those with children or elderly relatives, it was a very worrying time. By the time the Blitz was over in May 1941, over 40,000 civilians had been killed and more than 2 million people had lost their homes. Towns and cities had been changed overnight as familiar streets were turned into ruins. In one night the centre of Coventry, with its great cathedral, was destroyed and 554 people killed.

These children are sheltering in a trench and watching British and German planes fighting overhead during the Battle of Britain in 1940.

HELPING OUT

The danger and difficulties that everybody was facing brought people closer together. They soon made new friends in the shelters, and if a family was bombed out, other people would help them. Complete strangers crammed homeless mothers and children into their own cramped homes.

Women used their time in the shelters to write to their husbands and sons who were away fighting. They usually tried to sound cheerful in their letters and not give away their real feelings. But the men in the forces knew that the towns and cities were taking a terrible battering. In the end the Blitz made people more determined than ever to carry on and win the war.

(Above) This family was lucky, they escaped unhurt when a bomb exploded next to their Anderson shelter. The government was happy for this photograph to be taken.

(Below) The horror of war. Soldiers and Civil Defence workers looking for survivors after a bomb hit a school. The government would not allow this photograph to be printed in newspapers because it would have upset people.

This poster appeals to women to take jobs in the factories making the planes and weapons that were needed to fight the war.

Women played a really important part in winning the war. With so many men away in the armed forces, women were needed to take up the jobs the men had left behind. They were so important that in 1943 all the women between the ages of eighteen and fifty-one who had children to look after were required to do some kind of war service.

FACTORY WORKERS

Posters appealed to women to 'Come into the factories'. Millions of women were needed to help to build aeroplanes, tanks, ships and other military equipment. They took on kinds of skilled jobs that before the war had been done by men. It was the first time most of them had worked in a factory or even had a job outside the home.

WOMEN OF BRITAIN
COME INTO THE FACTORIES
ASK AT ANY EMPLOYMENT EXCHANGE FOR ADVICE AND FULL DETAILS

Many women were keen to help the war effort in this way, whilst the armed forces were actually fighting the enemy. But many women also needed the wages now that their husbands were away. However, women factory workers earned less than the men had. Because of the desperate need for weapons and equipment, factory workers often worked a twelve-hour shift. It seemed unfair to many women that when the war ended their jobs were given to returning **servicemen**, whether the women liked it or not.

It was difficult for women working long hours to look after their homes and children as well. For the first time many mothers had to let their children be looked after by a child-minder or go to a nursery. There were some people who did not approve of women taking on these jobs because they thought these mothers were neglecting their children.

During the war people got quite used to women bus conductors. Before the war, only men had jobs working on buses.

This painting by Dame Laura Knight shows a woman working as a skilled machinist. The war helped women to get jobs that, until then, had always been done by men.

'Go to it girls!' said the government. These ATS girls are on look-out duty for enemy planes. One of them is using a range-finder that helped the anti-aircraft guns hit their target.

Thousands of young women followed this advice and joined the ATS (Auxiliary Territorial Service) which was part of the army.

JOIN THE

ATS

ASK FOR INFORMATION AT THE NEAREST EMPLOYMENT EXCHANGE OR AT ANY ARMY OR ATS RECRUITING CENTRE

Women found it difficult to put their work before their families. However, the war did help men and women understand that there was no good reason why women should not do the same work as men.

WOMEN IN THE ARMED FORCES

At the start of the war, many women without children volunteered to join the armed forces. They became army nurses or lorry drivers, or operated the 'ack-ack' **guns** that were used against enemy aircraft. Some were in charge of look-out posts, keeping watch for enemy attacks. In the air force, women ran the airfield control rooms, whilst in the navy the **Wrens** kept radio contact with warships. Often these women soldiers and sailors were in danger, and some of them were killed, wounded or taken prisoner by the enemy.

Many women were on the Home Front during the heavy bombing. They took charge of air raid precautions (ARP), and in the fire service they braved the bombs to rescue people. Thousands joined the Women's **Land Army** to replace the farm workers who had gone away to fight, and without them the serious shortages of food would have been far worse.

One Land Girl, as they were called, remembers those days:

'A lot of people thought we were a bit of a joke to start with – city girls playing at being milk-maids and shepherdesses. But we all had a tremendous sense of purpose and we loved looking after the animals. On the farm where I worked, the farmer said we were the best help he had ever had.'

Many women from the towns joined the Women's Land Army to help produce food. Most of them had no experience of work on a farm. But their work was very important as they replaced farm workers who had joined the army.

CHILDREN AT WAR

Growing up during the war was really quite dull most of the time, but sometimes it could be very frightening. For the first time, children came face to face with death. Children didn't like the separation from their parents or the discomfort of air raid shelters. Not only did parents worry about the safety and happiness of their children, but children worried about their fathers and brothers who were away fighting. Some children did not see their fathers for five or six years. **Censorship** of letters and newspapers meant that they didn't even know where they were for most of the time. Some children were made orphans during the war.

School classes carried on during the war. The children in this class are practising wearing gas masks in case German planes dropped poison gas.

Gas masks were very uncomfortable. People were told to carry them at all times. However, poison gas was never dropped by the German bombers.

Even at school, children couldn't escape from the war. There were frequent air raid drills, and pupils had to practise using gas masks in case the Germans dropped poison gas. In the parks, children watched soldiers training. Beaches were out of bounds because barbed wire and explosive mines had been placed there for defence against possible attack.

'Got any chewing gum?' was the question children asked US soldiers. Sweets and chocolates were in short supply, but the American GIs always seemed to have some.

GIs

After the USA entered the war, thousands of American soldiers, **GIs**, came to Britain. Many were welcomed into English homes because they were away from their own families. Youngsters liked the 'Yanks', as they called them, because they gave them chocolate and chewing gum, which were in short supply. Many young women were keen to meet the GIs, who seemed glamorous in their smart uniforms when everything else in wartime Britain appeared drab and depressing. They taught the girls to dance the '**jitterbug**'.

ENTERTAINMENT

Because of the black-out most people stayed at home in the evenings. The new television service closed down at the start of the war, so everyone listened to the radio. For young children, 'Uncle Mac' was a hero. Every evening he introduced 'Children's Hour', and he always ended the programme with the words: 'Goodnight children – everywhere.' His programmes were a comfort to young people who were away from their own homes and missing their parents.

CHRISTMAS

Christmas in wartime was very different from the sort of Christmas people were used to. More than at any other time, families felt the pain of separation and remembered the good times before the war. Parents were unhappy that the war was spoiling the childhood of their children. For this girl, away from her parents, Christmas was the loneliest time of her life:

'My parents didn't come and see me. I think my father was probably away by then, and my mother simply didn't have the money for the fare. I felt I had been abandoned in favour of the new baby, and that I would never be wanted home again.'

People got most of their news and entertainment from the radio. They were always anxious to hear about the progress of the war. When they heard news of battles, people wondered whether their relatives had been in the fighting.

These Christmas shoppers are standing on sandbags to look at the toys. But even toys and sweets were difficult to buy at Christmas.

At Christmas, as during the rest of the year, the shops were almost empty. Although parents made a great effort to produce a Christmas morning surprise, all that most children found in their stocking was perhaps one orange, a small present and a few sweets. Sweets were still strictly rationed, and many of them had little flavour anyway. But people still decorated their homes, and even the underground stations and air raid shelters had decorations put up.

Father Christmas swaps his sleigh for a tank to bring a sack of toys for children visiting an American army camp.

WORKING FOR VICTORY

This poster showed peaceful British countryside to remind people what they were fighting for.

This poster showed peaceful British countryside to remind people what they were fighting for.

THE COGS

Everybody wanted to help bring the war to an end. Children wanted to play their part whilst their brothers and fathers were on the battlefields. However young they were, there were lots of jobs to be done. Younger children joined the 'Cogs', who were responsible for collecting any rubbish that could be useful. All kinds of scrap metal, such as old saucepans, could be melted down and used to make fighter aircraft. Waste paper was collected on a grand scale so that the government could produce yet more leaflets and posters urging people not to waste things, including paper!

SCOUTS AND GUIDES

Boy Scouts and Girl Guides were used for many important tasks such as building defences, keeping watch for fires during the bombing and helping at hospitals. Girls and boys knitted socks and gloves for soldiers, and teenagers became pen-pals to young soldiers and sailors. Boys who were not quite old enough to join the armed forces were able to serve in the Messenger Service. This tended to involve carrying messages for the army and being ready to go into action if telephone communications were broken down. During bombing raids, the older children cycled with urgent messages, and sometimes come home with badly-damaged bicycles.

At the age of 16, boys could become Air, Sea or Army cadets and begin military training. Girls could join the Girls' Training Corps or the Women's Junior Corps. The chance to wear a military uniform made these organizations very popular. In Germany, as they faced defeat, boys aged fourteen served as soldiers in some of the heaviest fighting.

These schoolboys are knitting scarves for soldiers. There were many ways in which children helped the war effort.

This boy is carrying a bathtub to a salvage dump. People handed in saucepans and even cut down iron garden railings. They thought it would all help to win the war.

(Right) Even when victory was in sight, help was still needed to bring in the harvest. Youngsters gave up their holidays and spare time to help the farmers.

Now that the war was over, couples such as this sailor and his girlfriend could begin to plan their lives again.

HOLIDAYS...
HARVEST DAYS...
HAPPY DAYS...

BRING IN THE
VICTORY HARVESTS

OCTOBER ··· MID·AUGUST & SEPTEMBER ··· END JULY-EARLY AUG

of POTATOES · GRAIN · FRUIT

ISSUED BY THE SCOTTISH EDUCATION DEPARTMENT & THE DEPARTMENT OF AGRICULTURE FOR SCOTLAND ·······

Working on the land was very important. All the year round families grew as much food as they could, and every bit of available land was planted. Youngsters helped out on local farms, particularly at harvest time, because there were very few farmworkers. School playing fields were turned into vegetable patches, and pupils worked hard on them after school and during the holidays.

Finally, nearly six years after it had started, the Second World War came to an end. Gradually the men and women in the armed forces began to return. They came back to find their towns and cities changed by the bombing and their children six years older. Many families had lost someone, and some children were now orphans. Husbands and wives, separated for such a long time, had to get to know each other again. The lives of some young women were going to be very different. Thousands had married GIs and set off to the USA. The people who survived the war were the lucky ones, but families had lost six years of their lives together.

A women's magazine gave this advice to its readers:

'Carry forward the grand things you have learned in your courageous war service and keep this new feeling of community living. Take it with you when the war is over to the building of a new world in which women share equally with men, so that it may be real and lasting.'

Peace at last. The soldiers come home to their families. This soldier has been a prisoner of war.

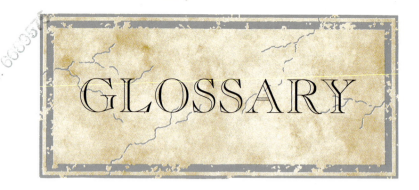

GLOSSARY

'ack-ack' guns Anti-aircraft guns.

Anderson shelters Small bomb shelters made of corrugated iron covered with earth which people had in their gardens.

Black-out No lights were allowed out of doors at night, and all windows were covered with heavy black material, so there was no light showing that would help enemy aircraft.

Blitz A shortened version of the German word *Blitzkrieg*, which meant 'lightning war'. It was used to describe the bombing of British cities.

Censorship Restricting what people read and write so that no important secrets are given away.

Civilians People who are not in the army, navy or airforce.

Conscripted People who are made to join the armed forces.

Emergency A sudden and dangerous situation that needs quick action.

Evacuation Moving people away from an area because of danger.

GI The name that was given to US soldiers. It actually means 'government issue'.

Home Front The towns and cities in Britain that were attacked by enemy aircraft.

Improvise To try to make things without the proper equipment.

'Jitterbug' A popular dance from the USA in the 1940s.

Land Army People who were organized to work on the farms.

Nazi Describes Germany under the leadership of Adolf Hitler, who was in power from 1933 to 1945.

Rationing Putting a limit on things such as food and clothes that people can buy so that everyone has a fair share.

Servicemen Members of the armed forces.

Slums Overcrowded houses in very poor condition.

Spy Someone who finds out information to help the enemy.

Wrens The Women's Royal Naval Service.

BOOKS TO READ

Rawcliffe, Michael, *Britain at War 1939-45* (B.T. Batsford, 1992)

Ross, Stewart, *The Home Front* (Wayland, 1990)

Smith, G, *How it was in the War* (Pavilion, 1989)

Westall, R, *Blitzcat* (Pan, 1990)

Yass, Marion, *The Home Front* (Wayland, 1971)

PLACES TO VISIT

Cabinet War Rooms, Clive Steps, King Charles Street, London SW1A 2AQ.
You can visit the underground rooms used by Winston Churchill during the Blitz.

Coventry Cathedral, Coventry, West Midlands.
You can see some remains of the cathedral that was bombed and exhibits about the Blitz.

D-Day Museum, Clarence Esplanade, Southsea, Hampshire PO5 3NT.
Sounds, images and everyday objects are used to recreate scenes of life in wartime Britain.

German Occupation Museum, Forest, Guernsey, Channel Islands.
This very interesting museum details life for British people in the Channel Islands after the Germans invaded them.

Imperial War Museum, Lambeth Road, London SE1 6HZ.
The most important war museum, with large displays that include life in wartime Britain.

The People's Palace, Glasgow Green, Glasgow, Scotland G40 1AT.
Their display shows the changes to ordinary Glaswegian life during the war.

Royal Air Force Museum, Grahame Park Way, Hendon, London NW9 5LL.
Britain's national museum of aviation has displays on the Battle of Britain, the Blitz and the Home Front.

Royal Engineers Museum, Prince Arthur Road, Gillingham, Kent.
They have a display that incudes a Home Front home.

Your local museum might well have exhibits about life during the war in your town.

INDEX

Figures in **bold** are illustrations. Glossary entries are shown by the letter g.